Cezanne Ryerson-Jodka

So You Want to Own a Horse...

A Wealth of Knowledge

This book is dedicated to the incredible horsemen I've had the privilege of learning from over the years. Thank You so much for the opportunities, you've taught me so much. I hope I can do your tutelage justice.

I love all of you.

Foreword

This book isn't about the beauty of horses or the wonderful times you will have riding through grassy fields.

This book is an honest, hard look at what it costs to own and take care of a horse. It's brutally honest. It's about the money, the time, the dedication to an animal that trusts you to take care of him.

The purchase price of a horse is nothing compared to the costs you will incur over time and if someone is willing to give you a free horse, well, as a well-known horse-man once told me: "There's no such thing as a free horse".

In this book I will try to give you an idea of what each of these expenses might cost but be aware, the area in which you live, other professionals opinions and charges and many other factors will play into the costs you will run into owning a horse.

Owning a horse is one of the most fulfilling hobbies in which you can participate. Horses are intuitive, intelligent and as I like to say 'Cheaper than therapy'.

Just keep in mind: Horses didn't ask for this life, we gave it to them, now it's up to us to do right by them no matter how hard the task.

That being said, lets get into the meat of the issue.

About The Author

A fourth generation horseman, Cézanne grew up learning Horsemanship from her grandmother and some of the "Old School" Trainers in San Diego such as Vicki Halsey (then Vance), Mercedes Cicliano, Wes Whitlock and other heavy hitters. Cézanne started her professional career with horses in Flynn Springs, California in 1983. Then as Ryan Quarter Horses she raised and broke colts and worked full time.

After being laid-off from her job in 1993 she went to work for a local carriage company driving Draft horses in the downtown area, going to school full time at night and continuing her own business on a smaller scale with her two young sons.

In 2000 Cézanne put her business on hiatus and went to work as the Breeding Manger for Sandy Arledge Quarter Horses and Far West Farms in Del Mar, California. As well as breeding and training award winning Quarter horse foals for Ms Arledge, she produced horse shows for the California Professional Horse Show Association and in the off season team roped on her favorite rope horse Doodle. In 2006 Far West Farms was sold and Cézanne worked for Vessels Stallion Farm as their Breeding Manager for a short time. She also worked as a vet assistant for a large animal vet in Rancho Santa Fe but in 2013 she missed running her own business so she revived it and changed the name to Challenger Quarter Horses in honor of the Challenger Shuttle crew.

Thirty-four years after beginning her adventure-filled professional life with horses and living her favorite quote; 'You're either in or in the way', you can find her in Aguanga, California with her husband and three Corgis bringing their grandson along as the sixth generation horseman in her family. She is still an avid team roper and team sorter and continues to breed quality American Quarter Horses, still breaks her own young horses and offers lessons to locals.

1

Buying a Horse

Common rule of thumb: People don't generally give away "good" horses.

As mentioned in the foreword, what you pay for a horse is a mere pittance to what you will pay over the lifetime of owning your horse.

The cost for a well-trained horse that is safe for a beginner will start around $6,500 depending on the market in your area at the time of purchase. A word of caution: don't get a rescue horse. Those horses are there for a reason and unless it's the type of rescue that rehabs horses and re-homes them (and won't object to you having the horse vetted), don't even consider them.

If someone wants to give you a horse, make sure you have it looked at by a veterinarian that can tell you if the horse is serviceable for the type of riding you want to do. A "retired show horse" may not be the best choice for trail riding as he has probably spent most of his life in an arena and would have no clue about how to act on the trail. Same goes the other way around, if you're buying a trail horse, don't expect him to do arena work unless you're willing to put in some time, and money, with a trainer.

Most "free" horses have some sort of issue. Your veterinarian will be able to tell you if it's soundness, behavior or health related. Those issues are not necessarily bad things depending on how severe but you want to make sure you have the resources, time and money, to take on that issue.

2

Housing Your Horse

You don't need a big, beautiful barn (he probably wont use it anyway).

Horses regulate their own body temperature in the Winter by the hair they grow and by the calories they burn. If they get cold, they walk to raise their body temperature and consume more hay. As long as you're "stoking the furnace" hence the term "Hay-burner", they're generally good to about -16F but but a good three sided run-in to get him out of the weather is a necessity.

A note regarding blankets: Have you ever seen a feral horse with a blanket on?

Unless your horse is showing and lives in a barn stall, he doesn't need a blanket. A blanket will flatten his hair coat and will actually make him colder. Especially in the rain. No matter how many blanket manufacturers tell you their blanket is "waterproof", it still gets wet on the inside from the horse sweating.

Bottom line: Horses don't need blankets.

Corrals

Whatever type of housing you choose for your new horse, it must be safe. It's not as easy as throwing up some chicken wire around a few t-posts. Your corral must be strong, safe and big enough to allow your horse to walk around and lie down comfortably.

A horse can pick up a corral just by putting his head through and walk around with it if it is not somehow anchored down. This may be amusing but when the horse gets his neck, head or legs caught in it and you get a look at your vet bill, it won't be funny anymore.

With costs being around $1500, a corral for a horse at home should be at least 24'x24' and be built with a good gauge pipe. There are many different gauges of pipe used by corral manufacturers but the most common are 1-5/8" and 1-7/8". The rails running horizontally on the panel

should be close enough together so as not
to allow the horse to put his head through.

Shelter

Whatever materials you use to build your horse his home, he absolutely needs a shelter of some sort. A well-built shelter will cost approximately $1,100. Wood is not a good choice because horses chew it. I've seen shelters fall on horses because the horse has chewed through a support. Metal is ideal.

Your horses shelter should have three sides so he can get in out of the wind. Wind is what makes horses cold so make sure you have a sturdy, safe shelter that faces north.

Fencing

There are several types of fencing material you can use to build your horses' enclosure. Don't scrimp on this material, your horses' life depends on it.

Lets look at a few, due to copyright laws I was unable to post photos of these fences but they are readily available with many examples on Google.

V-Mesh: This type of fencing is safe because if a horse somehow gets his feet on it, they won't go through. It also helps keep predators out. Make sure it's a heavy enough gauge to be safe. Material made from 12.5 and 14 gauge wire is best.

No-Climb or Square fence: Usually made from 12 or 14 gauge wire, this is a good fencing material as long as the squares are narrow (2"x4") to prevent the horse from getting his feet caught in it.

Welded Wire Panels: Usually made with 6 gauge wire with a 2"x4" opening, these panels are usually attached to a corral panel or posts of some sort.

Corral Panel: With many different styles of panel, the galvanized pipe corral is the most popular. If you choose this style, make sure the horizontal pipes are close enough to each other and of sufficient diameter that the horse can't get his head through. They can get stuck in these panels if the pipes are too far apart and break their neck.

PVC pipe or plastic fence, easily broken through, is not a good option to use as horse fence.

Wood is never a good choice as a material for horse fence. Horses chew wood and could get slivers stuck in their mouths or chew through a shelter support.

3

Feed

Forage is very important to your horses' diet, it keeps his hind gut working and his bowels moving.

You should never feed a horse strictly a pelleted (processed) diet. I've heard people say "There's less waste", well no, there's not less waste, it's still manure, it just takes on different form and still creates a mess when it rains if you don't pick it up.

There are many different types of forage available to feed your horse but his age, activity level and health play an integral role is determining which one to feed. It's best to consult your veterinarian but I will present the various types that are available here in Southern California.

Fed correctly, a horse will go through approximately a bale and a half per week at approximately 20 pounds per day. A lot of people feed their horses two times a day but horses are grazing animals and should have grass hay in front of them at all times. This helps prevent ulcers as horses are always producing stomach acid whether or not there is food in their stomach.

Hay prices fluctuate on a regular basis due to weather, fuel prices, quality and location. Currently I'm paying $16/bale for Teff hay. Teff is a grass that originated in Ethiopia as a grain. Lower in simple sugars and starches it's a great choice. Read more on Teff at TheHorse.com.

Alfalfa hay is a legume and an excellent source of protein, energy, calcium and other nutrients but low in fiber. There is much controversy among horsemen over the feeding of alfalfa hay but according to Anne Rodiek of CSU Fresno; "Its concentrations of protein and calcium meet the nutrient needs of horses in high levels of production, such as growth and lactation, but exceed the nutrient requirements of horses in other life stages." Talk to your vet before you feed alfalfa to make sure your horse can handle it. $18-20/bale.

Timothy hay with its relatively low protein, calcium and energy content (and highest price) is one of the bunch grasses for horses and since it's higher in fiber, is the most digestible and provides more chewing time for confined horses. $30/bale.

Bermuda grass is high in fiber making it an excellent choice for horses that are "easy keepers" since it satisfies the chewing instinct without adding extra calories. Its a great free feed grass to keep your horse busy chewing. $18-20/bale.

Orchard grass, while generally cheaper than timothy, is more expensive than bermuda or alfalfa but is a good choice. $20-23/bale.

Oat hay is one of my favorites although hard to find, for working horses. Some horses won't eat it because of the tough stalks.

You can read more about these hay feeds at Sweetwater Nutrition.

Prices are approximate and may be different in your area.

Your new horse may or may not need supplements depending on his work load and health. There are several supplements out there and some of them don't do a thing but drain your pocketbook. Be vigilant in your research before you spend the money on a supplement that you think he needs. Be sure to consult with your vet before you add any supplement or change your horses' forage. Changing feeds can adversely effect your horses gastrointestinal tract and cause colic. An issue we'll address in the next chapter.

There's an excellent article on vitamins and minerals for horses at DoctorRamey.com. Be sure to check out Dr. Ramey's other articles. He's a wealth of information.

4
Veterinarian

NOTE: I am not a veterinarian so I will only skim these issues. Please confer with your vet if you need more information.

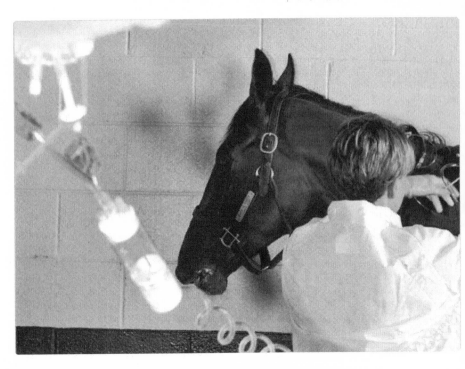

This is probably going to be one of the biggest holes in your budget when it comes to owning a horse. Well, maybe not, it's all expensive. A ranch call alone on average costs $50. Anything the vet does after that is extra.

Vaccinations & Deworming: Your vet can tell you which vaccinations are appropriate for your area and level of riding. If you ask ten horsemen how often you should vaccinate your horse you will get ten different answers. Best bet is to research the subject and form your own conclusions or just follow what your vet says.

Lameness: At some point in your horse ownership you will have to call your vet because your horse is limping. I had a vet tell me once; "If you don't see lameness in your horse at some point, you're doing it wrong". In other words, your horse doesn't go lame just standing in it's pen.

Some breeds are more susceptible to lameness due to inbreeding and/or genetic issues. This is why I pound into peoples skulls to have a horse vetted BEFORE you buy it. I can't even give you an estimate on a lameness exam but I've seen them run into the thousands depending on how far into the exam you want to go. There are x-rays, MRI, ultrasound and a multitude of treatments for lameness.

Colic: Colic is just another word for a belly ache in a horse. It can be caused by a number of things: hay changeover, excess supplement, or just plain stress. Colic can be the result of an impaction or gas. Impaction can be fatal if not treated quickly. The issue with gas is that it hurts and your horse can twist his gut rolling on the ground trying to move it through.

If your horse is laying down, rolling violently, not eating, sweating without exercise or stretching out, call your vet immediately. A vet call for colic can run in the thousands depending on how far you want to go in treating it.

Dental: Yes, your horse needs to have his teeth maintained. They continue to grow throughout his lifetime and if they're not maintained they can cause many different problems. A dental call averages $350.

Get to know your vet. They generally
don't mind questions and since they see
hundreds of horses a month they can
point you in the right direction if you
need advice on training or care.

5

Farrier

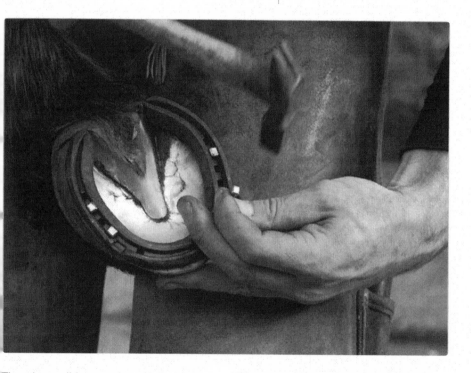

There is a well-known phrase in horseman-ship: "No Foot, No Horse" and it's true. Just like you, when a horses' feet hurt, he doesn't want to do anything.

There are several reasons a horses' feet might hurt that's why it's so important to have any horse you acquire looked at by a veterinarian BEFORE you pay for him or bring him home. Some hoof problems can be debilitating and end a horses' career or even his life and your hobby.

Horses need their feet "done" every six to eight weeks, give or take depending on his situation. This isn't an option, if you don't have his feet trimmed, they will grow out and become very uncomfortable for him.

Currently in my area just a trim costs on average $40. Shoes, which some horses absolutely need vary in price depending on the type of shoe he requires. The range is from $60 to sky's-the-limit. I've seen a set of shoes run $250 for a horse that need corrective shoes. I wish I could buy $250 shoes every six weeks!

6
Tack

Buy good quality tack, I call it "Heirloom tack", tack you'd want to leave to your kids. Your horses' comfort depends on it and ultimately your safety. A pain-ful horse will try to get away from pain and you may get caught up in the attempt.

22

The best tack is made from Hermann Oak leather or harness leather and the heavier weight leathers. There are some tack producers out there that are using cheap split leather or nylon. Don't buy it because it's cheap, you'll pay in the end...somehow.

Equipment you'll want to start out with would include:

- Halter

- Lead Rope

- Saddle

- Bridle

- Brush Box with brushes, hoof picks, combs and any other necessary grooming materials.

Halters are made from many different materials. Personally I use rope halters, I feel I get more control and they don't break as easily as nylon because there's no hardware involved. Nylon halters are okay, just make sure you get one that's made by a reputable maker. Hardware breaks, snaps break giving your horse the idea that he can get away just by pulling back hard enough. Dangerous in it-

self, you can be injured by flying hooves and hardware.

Lead Ropes are made from several materials as well. Avoid nylon, it will burn your hands if your horse decides to leave while you're leading him. Mohair is a good lead rope material and so is cotton. I prefer lead ropes without snaps, as I stated previously, they break too easily. If you use a good rope halter and lead properly you generally won't have any problems.

Saddles. Here's where people make the biggest mistakes when buying tack. I'm sure you've heard the phrase "You get what you pay for", this rings true with any tack. Keep that in mind.

Saddle fit is important, if your saddle doesn't fit your horse correctly you will cause him pain, and we all know where that goes. Don't buy a flex tree saddle, they flex all right, right down onto your horses withers. They were a cheap solution to an expense problem and created many other problems in the process. Buy a good saddle made by a reputable maker. Get help because you will need it. A good saddle will cost you anywhere from $500 to $5000 depending on the style, workmanship and materials.

The bridle is probably the most important piece of equipment you will have. Your horses' training level will dictate what type of bridle you'll buy so make sure you ask the person you're getting your horse from what type of bridle they were using. If they say "Oh, you can use anything on him", run away FAST. Again, don't buy nylon tack. A good bridle with a good bit can run $150-$200 or even more depending on your horses' training level.

7
Training

Everyone needs a coach some time.

You really should take a few lessons from a reputable trainer before you get your horse, this will tell you if riding is something you REALLY want to do or if it's just too much work. Believe me, it's a LOT of work. I've seen too many horses sit and rot in a yard because they THOUGHT they wanted to ride. It's not at all fair to the horse.

I still take lessons from other horse trainers when I feel like I'm having an issue or when I want a refresher.

Training for your horse can run anywhere from $600 a month and up depending on what discipline you're interested in and the area in which you live.

If you need to board your horse while you're in training that can cost around $800 a month. Of course there are many other factors that could run these numbers up or down.

8

Transportation

If you can't afford a rig, you can't afford a horse.

This is, in my opinion, one of the most important points. You should be able to transport your horse no matter where you live or even if your horse is boarded.

You need a sturdy, safe trailer and a vehicle that can pull and stop it. I've seen many people buy a trailer and try to pull it with a sub standard vehicle. It pulled the

trailer okay but when it came to stopping it
there was a BIG problem.

Don't depend on others to move your
horse during an emergency. They don't
know your horse, your horse doesn't know
them. I'm sure you see the problem here.
I've moved dozens of horses during fires
that people didn't have the means to move
on their own. It's not fair to the horse and
not fair to the person who ends up rescu-
ing him either.

Make sure your horse will load. There's
nothing like trying to load a horse when
the flames are running towards you.

There are many horse trailer manufacturers
out there, make sure you get one made by
a reputable maker. If you buy used, have a
professional look it over BEFORE you buy
it. Your horses' life depends on it. A good,
sturdy trailer will cost anywhere from
$5000 up.

9
It's a Big Job

Owning a horse is mucking pens, grooming muddy horses, keeping track of health
maintenance, making sure you're home to
feed at a regular time every day, feeding in
the dark, rain and cold, calling the vet at

2am when your horse is down, arranging
for someone to take care of your horse
while you go on vacation (if you can still
afford a vacation), worrying that your horse

might be lame and keeping up with a regular exercise program.

If you have any doubt in your mind about
being able to afford to keep a horse, don't.
I've seen too many neglected horses because the owner lost interest. I went to a
sale in Arizona a few years ago and when I
came out to leave someone had tied a sad-
dled horse to my trailer with a note:
'Please take my horse, I can't afford him
any more'. Don't do that.

Think long and hard before you take on the
responsibility of a horse.

Good Luck and Happy Trails!

Made in the USA
Columbia, SC
22 February 2024

32186234R00019